Welcome to the music

From James Fountain

I grew up surrounded by music. Both my mother and father played in the local Salvation Army brass band and I first picked up the cornet at the age of three. As a youngster, I played with my local brass band, The GUS Band, The National Youth Brass Band of Great Britain and then the Grimethorpe Colliery Band. I then went on to study trumpet at the Guildhall School of Music and Drama in London.

Like many other trumpet players, I am constantly listening to recordings of great players. Check out Wynton Marsalis, Håkan Hardenberger and Sergei Nakariakov. However, one of my brass-playing icons is Maurice Murphy, former Principal Trumpet at the London Symphony Orchestra. His thrilling playing stretches across the LSO on countless film soundtracks and other amazing recordings. It was one of the main reasons I became a trumpet player!

James Fountain, Principal Trumpet, LSO

From Sir Simon Rattle

Following the publication of the delightful *How To Build an Orchestra,* I'm thrilled to introduce you to *The Little Book of the Orchestra* series which offers a remarkable and entertaining insight into the instruments of the orchestra.

The London Symphony Orchestra's goal is to bring the greatest music to the greatest number of people. This is at the heart of everything that it does and has done for over 100 years. Established in 1904 by a number of London's finest musicians, the LSO is still owned by its members, 95 brilliant musicians who come from around the world.

The work of LSO Discovery, the orchestra's community and education programme, is something to which all of us are particularly committed. It brings the work of the LSO together with all parts of society and engages with many people who would not otherwise have the opportunity to interact with music. Its goals are embodied in our regular schools and family concerts.

The Little Book of the Orchestra series is a further extension of the LSO's aims to make and share music with many. I hope that by reading it and listening to the music, you will discover the true magic that music brings to all our lives.

Enjoy.

Sir Simon Rattle, Music Director, LSO

Contents

The trumpet calls	4
Blowing and buzzing	6
Pressing the valves	8
Marching forward	10
Finding a voice	12
An orchestra audition	14
A family of trumpets	16
In the recording studio	18
Varying the sound	20
At the rehearsal	22
Playing live	24
The opening night	26
Part of the orchestra	28
More about the music	30
Glossary	31
Index	32

Look out for panels with suggestions of music to listen to. You can find this music played by the LSO and its members to download online at www.lso.co.uk/alb/Trumpet.

The trumpet calls

The Moon and the Earth fill the huge cinema screen. And the music fills the room. Three clear notes on the trumpet begin a spectacular welcome to the Sun.

LISTEN to the start of *Also Sprach Zarathustra (So Said Zarathustra)* by Richard Strauss (1). Look out for the three clear notes played by the trumpets at the beginning. Then they are joined by other brass instruments.

As the film ends, people start to leave. But not Peter, his head is still buzzing. He decides he will learn the trumpet and, one day, play music like that.

- The sound of trumpets is good for greeting an important person – or an important event like the sunrise.

- Trumpets are popular in film music because they can create a sense of excitement.

- You blow a trumpet to make a sound.

- Trumpets are usually made of brass. They are part of the brass family of instruments.

Blowing and buzzing

Peter starts to learn the trumpet. Over the next few years, he has lessons at school but practises at home. It is not easy. Blowing a trumpet is about buzzing the lips and breath control.

- A trumpet player buzzes (or vibrates) his lips into a trumpet's mouthpiece. It's like blowing a raspberry without using the tongue. The buzz makes the trumpet's sound.

- He can change the pitch – how high or low the sound is – by changing his buzz.

Peter practises buzzing in the mirror. He keeps his lips firm and straight, as though he's saying 'M'.

- A player learns the right mouth shape and way of buzzing. This is called his embouchure.

◎ Sound wobbles – or vibrates – through the air. In a trumpet, the buzz vibrates down the trumpet and out of its bell.

Peter puts the trumpet to his lips – not too hard – and buzzes again into the mouthpiece. His buzz moves through the trumpet.

◎ The instrument amplifies the buzz (makes it louder) and changes how it sounds.

Peter practises and practises. He controls his breath and tuts his tongue to separate the notes. His sound gets clearer and his notes stronger.

LISTEN to the sound of a trumpet player buzzing without his trumpet. Next hear him blowing into the trumpet mouthpiece only and then into the whole trumpet. Notice how changing his buzz changes the pitch (2).

Pressing the valves

Peter doesn't just use his buzz to change the pitch. He can press down the trumpet's three valves in different ways to play different notes, too.

◎ A trumpet is a curled up, hollow tube of brass. The curled tube makes it easier to hold.

◎ A standard-sized trumpet tube is nearly 1.5 m long.

Mouthpiece

Valve

Bell

Pipe/tube

◎ Pressing down the valves changes the length of the trumpet's tube. This allows a trumpeter to play more notes, giving the instrument a larger range.

As Peter learns to play the trumpet, he also learns its history.

Early trumpets only played a few notes – great for greetings and sending signals in battle. Over 3,000 years ago, the ancient Egyptian Pharaoh Tutankhamun had trumpets.

Much later, better brass trumpets were made. With these, expert trumpeters found ways of playing more notes, mostly just by changing their buzzing.

By the 17th and 18th centuries, composers wrote lots of challenging trumpet music.

In the 19th century, orchestras got bigger and the music they played more complex. Now came trumpets with valves, that easily played all the notes a composer wanted. The trumpet became ever more popular, in orchestras, dance bands and alongside a piano.

LISTEN to 'The Trumpet Shall Sound' from *The Messiah* by G F Handel. It was first performed in 1742 (3). Then a modern trumpet plays a chromatic scale from high to low, showing its range of notes (4).

9

Marching forward

Peter plays the trumpet more and more. He joins his school's orchestra. He loves the sound of the other brass instruments.

He sometimes plays the cornet as well as the trumpet. He plays this with a band that marches down the street for a local festival.

- There are many other instruments made of brass. Like the trumpet, they are played by buzzing into a mouthpiece.

- Each brass instrument has its own type of sound. The big tuba plays the lowest notes.

- An orchestra has a brass section, along with strings, woodwind and percussion.

LISTEN to the *Fanfare for the Latin-American Allies* by Henry Cowell (5), arranged purely for brass and percussion. Imagine playing this as you marched down the street.

Tuba

Cornet

Finding a voice

Peter's dream does not change. He is going to be a professional trumpet player. He studies hard and practises more. His teacher encourages him to go to music college.

At home, he listens to all sorts of trumpet music – and plays along! He is clever at copying what he hears. But what sort of trumpeter should he be?

Shall he be a cool-cat jazz player?

Should he dance to the big-band sound?

He could add rhythm to disco and pop. He'd get to meet lots of stars.

LISTEN to some extracts from this brass arrangement by Eric Crees from *West Side Story* by Leonard Bernstein: jazzy sounds in 'Cool – Fugue' (6), then get into some dance music in 'Maria' (7). And can you see why brass can add a strong rhythm in 'America' (8)?

An orchestra audition

Peter remembers the film music he loved. It was played by a symphony orchestra. At college he takes his trumpet skills still higher – and plays in as many orchestras as possible.

> A large symphony orchestra's repertoire – the range of music it plays – is huge. It includes music from the 18th century to today.

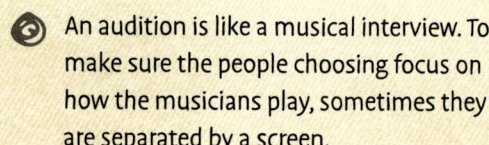

> An audition is like a musical interview. To make sure the people choosing focus on how the musicians play, sometimes they are separated by a screen.

Orchestral music today can be for concert performance, films, TV or computer games.

When Peter leaves college, he has a chance to audition for a big orchestra. He is shaking with nerves on the day. It is strange playing to people hidden behind a screen.

But all that passion, playing and practising pays off. He is in!

LISTEN to three trumpets play in beautiful harmony at the start of this extract from Gustav Mahler's Symphony No. 3 (9). Slowly, the whole orchestra joins in building a gorgeous end. Mahler wrote passionate music for huge orchestras.

A family of trumpets

Peter loves his new job. He sits in the brass section, next to the other two trumpet players. Annette, the principal trumpeter, helps Peter settle in. She leads the trumpets and plays some brilliant solos.

Together, the players bring a lot of colour to the music. They use mutes to vary the sound and sometimes play other instruments from the trumpet family.

- Sometimes composers write for the flugelhorn or the cornet. A trumpet player will play these too.

- There are different sized trumpets. The piccolo trumpet is the smallest. It plays some very high notes.

- A mute fits into the bell of a trumpet. It changes the sound the trumpet makes.

- There are lots of different shaped mutes which make different sounds.

LISTEN to the snarly trumpets played with mutes in 'Prelude, Fugue and Riffs' by Leonard Bernstein (10). And, in these extracts from the trumpet concerto *From the Wreckage* by Mark-Anthony Turnage, the solo trumpet player starts the piece on a flugelhorn (11), then moves to a standard trumpet (12) and finishes on a piccolo trumpet (13).

Straight mute

Other mutes

Cornet

In the recording studio

Peter's days are filled with rehearsals and concerts. Before long though, he finds himself in a recording studio, playing a film score.

Peter keeps his eyes peeled on the conductor. She also composed the music. The orchestra's timing has to be very exact to fit the action of the film.

- The conductor shows the musicians when to start playing and the feeling she wants them to create with the music.

- She sees the film on a small screen to help to fit the music to the moving images.

- Musicians may wear 'cans' (big headphones) for recording. Through these, they hear timed clicks. These clicks help them play in time together very accurately.

- A crew of sound engineers operate the recording equipment.

LISTEN to this piece of music written by Ron Goodwin for the film *633 Squadron* (14). Imagine aeroplanes flying off to a battle in the sky accompanied by this heroic brass sound.

Varying the sound

It's tricky recording a film score. The musicians are seeing the music for the first time. There's no chance to practise first. It's essential they sight-read music very well.

The composer clearly loves the trumpet. She uses all its colourful sounds. As she conducts, Peter and the other trumpet players show off their skills.

She writes a high, tricky trumpet melody as the hero hunts the baddy …

She asks for flutter-tonguing, a 'frrr-frrr' sound, when the baddy appears …

A soft note gets suddenly loud at a dramatic moment. That requires a lot of breath control!

LISTEN to the different sounds you can create on the trumpet from a high, exciting melody (15), a flutter-tongued moment of suspense (16), a dramatic crescendo (17) and a bit of humour (18).

There's even a funny moment. The composer can't resist a 'wah-wah' sound made by a hand cupped over a mute.

21

At the rehearsal

Soon the orchestra is back at a rehearsal with Leo, their main conductor. Their next concert will be broadcast live and recorded. As they rehearse, the sound engineers adjust equipment and prepare for the performance.

Live concerts are often broadcast around the world on the radio and the Internet.

Engineers try to capture the mix of sounds, loud and soft, high and low, that the audience in the concert hall hears.

"We're going for drama tonight," says Leo. "We will start with women warriors riding through the sky and end with a trip to the movies! Brass, are you ready to conjure up the Valkyries?"

LISTEN to 'The Ride of the Valkyries' (19) from The Ring cycle of operas by Richard Wagner. Do you recognise it? Can you imagine it being used in a film?

- Dramatic orchestral music has inspired the music for many films. Film scores now form part of a symphony orchestra's repertoire.

- Composers like Dimitri Tiomkin (1894–1979) and John Williams (1932-) have helped make films memorable for their music.

The concert finishes with some of the film music by Dimitri Tiomkin. The brass work hard – and the audience are swept away, too. They don't even need pictures to feel the magic of the movies!

🎵 Then a big-nosed man falls in love ...

🎵 And, to end, a heroic battle.

LISTEN to excerpts from Dimitri Tiomkin's music for the following films: *Circus World* (20), *Rawhide* (21), *Cyrano de Bergerac* (22) and *The Alamo* (23 and 24), with its beautiful trumpet solo.

The opening night

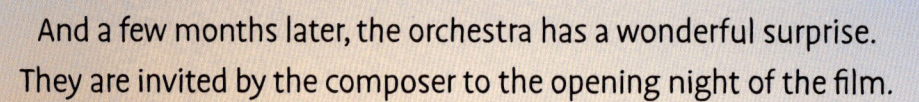

And a few months later, the orchestra has a wonderful surprise. They are invited by the composer to the opening night of the film.

Peter settles down to watch the film with his friends. As it begins, he hears the trumpets play and he smiles. His dream really has come true!

Part of the orchestra

This is a pictogram of a full-sized orchestra, such as the London Symphony Orchestra. You can see where the trumpets usually sit and the other players. There are no real rules about the size and make up of an orchestra. The instruments and number of players change from piece to piece.

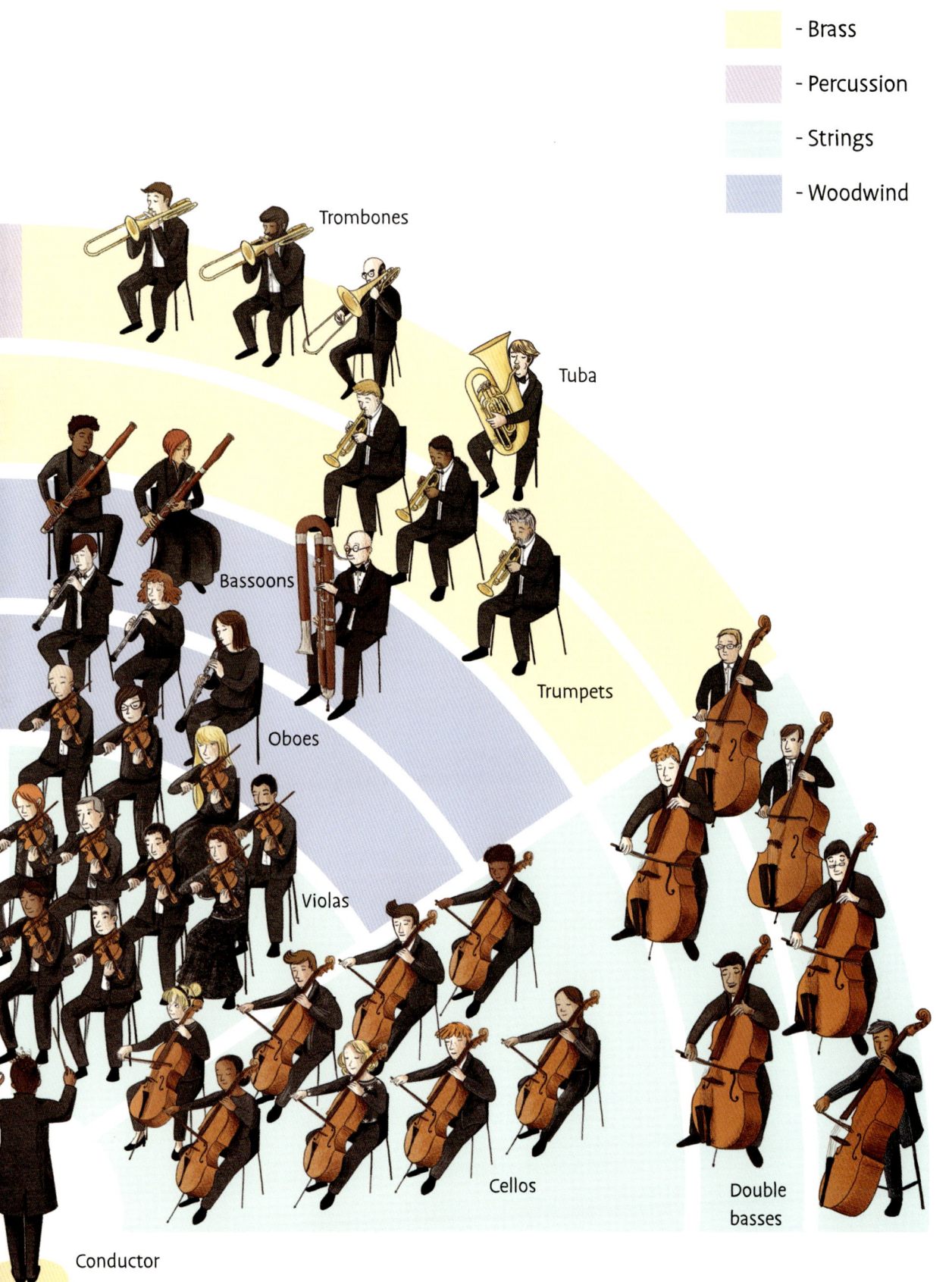

More about the music

The tracks recorded specially for this book are performed by Niall Keatley, Trumpet, LSO. All the rest are performed by the London Symphony Orchestra.

Track 1: *Also Sprach Zarathustra* (So Said Zarathustra) by Richard Strauss (1864–1949). Strauss called the opening of this 1896 piece 'Sunrise'. It has often been used in films and TV programmes linked to space.
Track 2: Niall buzzes three times: firstly without a trumpet, secondly with a trumpet mouthpiece and thirdly with the whole trumpet.
Track 3: 'The Trumpet Shall Sound', *The Messiah* (1741), by George Frideric Handel (1685–1759). A trumpeter and singer show off their skills in this famous duet.
Track 4: Niall plays across the full range of the trumpet, moving up from one of the lowest notes to one of the highest.
Track 5: *Fanfare for the Latin-American Allies* by Henry Cowell (1897–1965), arrange by Eric Crees (1952–). This 1942 piece celebrates the people of Latin America who were supporting the USA during the Second World War.
Track 6: 'Cool – Fugue', *West Side Story*, by Leonard Bernstein (1918–1990), arranged by Eric Crees (1952–). First performed in 1957, the musical *West Side Story* is famous for its mix of different styles of music (see also tracks 7 and 8). This version of 'Cool' uses lots of jazzy effects.
Track 7: 'Maria', *West Side Story*, by Leonard Bernstein (1918–1990), arranged by Eric Crees (1952–). This instrumental song 'Maria' plays up its strong cha-cha rhythm. The cha-cha is a Cuban dance.
Track 8: 'America', *West Side Story*, by Leonard Bernstein (1918–1990), arranged by Eric Crees (1952–). Musicians have to count very carefully when playing this famous song's tricky rhythm.
Track 9: Symphony No. 3 in D Minor, Mvt 6 by Gustav Mahler (1860–1911). Completed in 1896, this is the last part of a very long symphony. Mahler described the movement as 'What Love Tells Me' and asked for musicians to play it with deep feeling.
Track 10: 'Prelude, Fugue and Riffs', Mvt 1 by Leonard Bernstein (1918–1990), arranged by Eric Crees (1952–). We hear the start of 'Prelude' (which means introduction), the opening of this 1949 piece. Bernstein wanted to link jazz with some of the traditions of classical music.
Tracks 11, 12 and 13: *From the Wreckage* by Mark-Anthony Turnage (1960–). The composer uses the three different types of trumpet to show a progress of emotions, through darkness and pain to calm and understanding.
Track 14: *633 Squadron* by Ron Goodwin (1925–2003). This is the main theme for the 1964 film about a heroic squadron of aeroplanes fighting in the Second World War.
Tracks 15, 16, 17 and 18: Niall plays music written by Rachel Leach (1973–) especially for this book. The first track is a scene-setting melody that brings a sense of mystery and excitement. The other three show off some of the effects a skilled trumpet player can achieve.
Track 19: 'The Ride of the Valkyries' from *The Valkyrie*, the second of The Ring cycle, four linked operas by Richard Wagner (1813–1883). This famous music, often used in film and TV, was first performed in 1870. The Valkyries were women warriors from Viking myth, who rode through the sky on horses to carry heroes who died in battle to heaven.
Track 20: 'The John Wayne March', *Circus World* by Dimitri Tiomkin (1894–1979). Russian born, American composer Dimitri Tiomkin wrote the music for many famous films and was nominated for 22 Academy Awards (Oscars) for his work, winning four of them. He worked in a huge variety of styles. This first example was written for the 1964 film *Circus World* about a travelling circus. It starred John Wayne.
Track 21: Theme to *Rawhide* by Dimitri Tiomkin, lyrics by Ned Washington. This song is the theme tune for a popular US TV series about cowboys, which was first shown between 1959 and 1965.
Track 22: Overture to *Cyrano de Bergerac* by Dimitri Tiomkin. This music was written for a 1950 version of the famous romantic story about a brilliant soldier, Cyrano de Bergerac, who thinks no one will love him because of it.
Tracks 22-23: *The Alamo Suite* by Dimitri Tiomkin. A 1960 film, *The Alamo,* tells the story of the heroic defence of the Alamo fortress in Texas, USA, in 1836. The Texan forces, led by Davy Crockett, were defeated by the Mexican army.

Glossary

amplifies – makes louder
audition – like an interview, a formal meeting where a musician plays to show off their skill to win a job
bell – the bottom end of a brass instrument that flares outwards to form a bell-like shape
big-band – describes the style of music linked to large bands of brass and percussion instruments. Big bands became popular in the 1940s and 1950s
brass – the name of the family of wind instruments usually made of brass; brass is made from two metals, copper and zinc, mixed together
broadcast – send out an event or information by radio, television or the web
chromatic – describes a scale in Western music that uses every note as it goes up and down
composer – someone who writes, or composes, music
concerto – a piece for orchestra and usually one soloist (often in three movements)
conductor – the person who directs an orchestra or choir
crescendo – gradually getting louder
embouchure – the mouth shape a musician forms to play a brass or other type of wind instrument
fanfare – a short, dramatic melody, usually played on a brass instrument, originally used to send signals across wide spaces
film score – music written to go with a film
flutter-tonguing – a playing technique where a musician flutters their tongue, blowing a 'frrr-frrr' sound into a wind instrument
fugue – a musical structure, like a very complex round, where several players all play the same melody but start at different times and then develop the ideas separately
jazz – a type of music that originated in the African-American community in the early 20th century. It often features swing rhythms, 'blues' harmonies and improvisation (musicians making it up on the spot!)
melody – a line of musical notes that makes a satisfying shape, or a musical sentence, sometimes called the tune

mouthpiece – the part of a musical instrument placed on or near the mouth
movement – one section of a larger piece; often shortened to Mvt in music description
mute – a device that fits inside the bell of brass instruments used to change or quieten the sound
opera – a drama set to music, with the words sung
overture – an instrumental piece, often an introduction to a larger work
percussion – the family of instruments that you generally hit or shake to make a sound
pitch – sound described as high or low
principal – in an orchestra, describes the lead player of a particular instrument whose part in the music may include solo sections
range – the notes an instrument can play
recording studio – a place with special equipment for recording and mixing sound
rhythm – a collection of notes of different duration forming a pattern
scale – notes played up or down in pitch order
sight-read – playing music for the first time by reading it from the page without practising beforehand
solo – a prominent part played by one musician alone
sound engineer – a person who deals with the technical details of recording or broadcasting music
strings – the family of musical instruments that uses strings to make their sound
suite – a collection of pieces, played as a group
symphony – a large piece for an orchestra (often in four movements)
valve – a type of button or lever on a brass instrument that is pressed to change its pitch
vibrate – to wobble very fast
volume – how loud or quiet a sound is
woodwind – the family of wind instruments originally made of wood

31

Index

auditions 14–15

big-bands 13
brass 4–5, 10–11, 13, 16–17, 23, 25, 28–29
buzzing 6, 7, 9, 10

concerts 18, 22–25
conductors 18–19, 22
cornet 10, 11, 16–17

disco music 13

embouchure 6, 7, 8

film music 4–5, 14–15, 18–27
flugelhorn 16–17

jazz 12–13

making a sound 5–10, 20–21
music pieces
   633 *Squadron* (R Goodwin) 19
   Also Sprach Zarathustra (R Strauss) 4–5
   Fanfare for the Latin-American Allies
   (H Cowell) 11
   From the Wreckage (M-A Turnage) 17
   Overture to *Cyrano de Bergerac*
   (D Tiomkin) 25
   'Prelude, Fugue and Riffs' (L Bernstein) 17
   Symphony No. 3 (G Mahler) 15
   The Alamo Suite (D Tiomkin) 25
   'The John Wayne March' (D Tiomkin) 25
   'The Ride of the Valkyries' (R Wagner) 23
   'The Trumpet Shall Sound' (G F Handel) 9
   Theme from *Rawhide* (D Tiomkin) 25
   West Side Story (L Bernstein/E Crees) 13

orchestra
   recording sessions 18–23
   rehearsals 18–19, 22–23
   sections of an orchestra 28–29

percussion 11, 28–29
pitch 6,
pop music 13

strings 11, 28–29

trumpet
   family 16–17
   mouthpiece 6, 7, 8, 10
   parts of 8
   piccolo 16–17
   using a mute 16–17, 21

woodwind 11, 28–29

About the LSO

The LSO was formed in 1904 as London's first self-governing orchestra and has been resident orchestra at the Barbican since 1982. It is the world's most recorded symphony orchestra and has appeared on some of the greatest classical recordings and film soundtracks. The LSO also runs LSO Discovery, its ground-breaking education programme that is dedicated to introducing the finest music to young and old alike and lets everyone learn more from the orchestra's players.

For more information on the London Symphony Orchestra, please visit www.lso.co.uk

First published in Great Britain in 2023 by Wayland
Copyright © Hodder and Stoughton, 2023
Illustrations copyright © Hodder and Stoughton, 2023
Text copyright © Hodder and Stoughton, 2023
Introduction © Sir Simon Rattle and James Fountain, 2023
Music in accompanying CD and download © LSO LIVE LTD

All rights reserved.

Wayland, an imprint of
Hachette Children's Group
Part of Hodder and Stoughton
Carmelite House
50 Victoria Embankment
London EC4Y 0DZ

An Hachette UK Company
www.hachette.co.uk
www.hachettechildrens.co.uk

ISBN 978 1 5263 1472 7 HB
ISBN 978 1 5263 1473 4 PB

Printed in Dubai

Design by Peter Scoulding
Edited by Rachel Cooke and Paul Rockett
Music consultancy by Rachel Leach on behalf of the London Symphony Orchestra
Thanks, too, to Philip Cobb, formerly Principal Trumpet, LSO, and my godson Peter Holmes, trumpeter and composer